A Century
of
Sonnets

BOOKS BY
JAMES A. MICHENER

Tales of the South Pacific
The Fires of Spring
Return to Paradise
The Voice of Asia
The Bridges at Toko-Ri
Sayonara
The Floating World
The Bridge at Andau
Hawaii
Report of the County Chairman
Caravans
The Source
Iberia
Presidential Lottery
The Quality of Life
Kent State: What Happened and Why
The Drifters
A Michener Miscellany: 1950-1970
Centennial
Sports in America
Chesapeake
The Covenant
Space
Poland
Texas
Legacy
Alaska
Journey
Caribbean
The Eagle and the Raven
Pilgrimage
The Novel
The World Is My Home: A Memoir
James A. Michener's Writer's Handbook
Mexico
Creatures of the Kingdom
My Lost Mexico
Literary Reflections
Recessional
Miracle in Seville
This Noble Land: My Vision for America
A Century of Sonnets

with A. Grove Day
Rascals in Paradise

with John Kings
Six Days in Havana

A Century
of
Sonnets

by

James A. Michener

Published in celebration of
James A. Michener's
90th Birthday

State House Press
Austin, Texas
1997

Library of Congress Cataloging-in-Publication Data

Michener, James A. (James Albert), 1907-
A century of sonnets / by James A. Michener.
p.   cm.
ISBN 1-880510-50-2 (clothbound : alk. paper)
ISBN 1-880510-51-0 (ltd ed. : alk. paper)
1. Sonnets, American. I. Title.

PS3525.I19C45 1997   96-54228
811'.54—dc21

Printed in the United States of America

cover design by David Timmons

STATE HOUSE PRESS
P.O. Box 15247
Austin, Texas 78761

Table Of Contents

Great Music Filled The Crannies Of My Soul

To Watch This Flow Of Life Has Been Most Thrilling

Bound In Gallant Brotherhood Together

I Owe The World

The Church Stands Central

Simple Truths That Reign Eternally

Preface

This collection of highly personal sonnets was assembled over a period of seven decades. It contains a few poems in other forms, but together they comprise the portrait of a boy in a rural Pennsylvania town who had immersed himself in classical literature, especially the sonnets of Shakespeare, Milton, Keats and Wordsworth.

My first sonnet, which literally exploded in my mind with such force that I knelt in a blinding rainstorm and prayed, came in 1927 when I was a college student, alert as always to the grandeurs and subtleties of nature. That it should have expressed itself in iambic pentameters was to be expected, for I had made that felicitous form my predilected favorite. I have always thought in iambics, intuitively voicing them as I take my evening walks.

JAMES A. MICHENER
Austin, Texas
1996

-1-

Today the long drought ended and the rain,
Descending like an answer to a prayer,
Came back to make the land take heart again.
How dreadful when the land was bleak and bare
And corn stood withered in the torrid blast,
Beef cows were led away to needless slaughter
And housewives in their kitchens stood aghast
When pipes delivered sediment not water.

Now comes the rain! With face upraised to heaven
I feel the raindrops mingle with my tears,
And though an infidel I am sore driven
To kneel and thank the gods who through the years
Have kept close watch upon this precious soil
Through drought and flood and freeze and endless toil.

———————

My first sonnet, composed in 1927 while hitchhiking from
Chester, Pennsylvania, to Swarthmore College.

Most of all I loved my occupation

The sonnet is an elegant invention
For disciplining thought and fey confession.
Its structure expedites its main intention
Which is: 'Move thought in orderly progression.'
Lines five through eight quite often will decide
The merits of the verse and its fruition,
But only if new concepts can provide
Fresh insights to avoid mere repetition.
The third quatrain is saved for affirmation
In forms so bold there can be no confusion,
With evidence attesting approbation
All leading to a powerful conclusion.
    The last two lines must not be squandered lightly,
    They should be used to summarize most tightly.

The human brain is geared to run on iambs
That stately measure which Will Shakespeare used.
A chain of iambs wanders by like shy lambs
Pursuing rules that cannot be abused.
They function best when in a group of five
Pentameter it's called in such formation.
On its skilled use the abler poets thrive,
Composing verse with strict configuration.
Pope ridiculed iambs in apt quotation:
'And ten short words march forth in one dull line.'
Yet poets of exalted reputaton
Have said: 'This trusted meter fits me fine.'
  But still, short-longs in deadly repetitions
  Make lesser poets sound like mathematicians.

How great the English poets seem today,
Their works a balm for all our human needs:
The evening solitude of Thomas Gray,
The brassy clash of Kipling's Asian breeds,
Staid Wordsworth, restless with his time's malaise,
While Pope lurks with his deadly acid quill,
Keats sings the beauty of lost classic days
And Browning mourns his graveyard on the hill.
Great Shakespeare stands alone, a soul apart
With mind of universal scope and power.
John Milton probed his era's soul and heart,
Yet speaks today to matters of this hour.
   Philosophers and nations gape in wonder
   Their minds set blazing by these poets' thunder.

————

The graveyard passage, from Robert Browning's *A Grammarian's Funeral*, has haunted me. It returns in Sonnet 36.

ODE TO TENNYSON

The furies play about your whitened head
  And drop away in mortal anguish tried
For they have naught to do with living dead

Nor with the aging many who have sighed
  And with old tears bewailed an ancient past.
No furies touch your pages; life has died

Before it sees your fingertips, and fast
  Into the realms of immortality
Your painless, tiring music fades. At last

The old senescence dips into the sea
  Of your half-tiresome tears and leaves the earth
No richer and no poorer. It would be

Salvation to your soul if honest mirth,
  Or ugly gentleness, or full-mouthed gales
Of laughter played on your white, empty birth,
  To give the passion that retreats and pales.

———

Written in 1931 after I had become bored from teaching
him for some time.

The pines of Bowdoin form a noble throng,
And in their dim and lovely speckled light
Longfellow strolled and framed his gentle song:
'I heard the trailing fragments of the Night
'Sweep through her marble halls.' Such limpid phrases
Made him the nation's predilected bard,
Modest receptor of the whole world's praises.
Two other bright and gifted youths worked hard:
Nat Hawthorne whose words critical and spare
Would be addressed to problems of the soul,
And Franklin Pierce, a shy lad who would dare
To choose the Presidency as his goal.
    All from this little college with traditions,
    That scholars must pursue their high ambitions.

Bowdoin, a fine small college founded in 1794 in Bruns-
wick, Maine, is pronounced 'Bow-d'n.'

-7-

The touchstone of my life was loyalty
To any task for which I volunteered.
I did not pledge to local royalty
But to the common good that I revered.
Those who employed me found an eager man,
Not limited to short eight-hour day,
Who kept his eye upon the master plan
And strove to edge it forward on its way.
I loved my school, my team, my Navy station,
My state, my country and the human race,
But most of all I loved my occupation:
The task of writing with insight and grace.
  In time I learned the way to help my nation
  Was to excel within my own vocation.

I believe that this sonnet comes closest to defining the real me. I exerted a passionate loyalty in all I did or tried to do.

-8-

Each night I walk she greets me with a smile
This crippled woman with the damaged brain:
'I'm glad to see you hike your steady mile,
'It's good to hear that you're at work again.'
She vaguely understands I publish books
And badgered one from me to show the town.
I see her in the mall in quiet nooks
My book in hand, but reading upside down.
I think that we are judged by how we use
Whatever gifts we are vouchsafed by God.
Allowed my brain, she might have reached the stars.
Entrapped by hers, I'd leave my paths untrod.
   For her I merely mark the end of day,
   For me she flames a beacon for my way.

A sonnet first published in *Literary Reflections* in 1993 as
part of a larger poem.

-9-

A writer ought to go against the grain,
He should not seek a meaningless applause
Or meretricious economic gain,
His art should fortify a nobler cause.
He is the spokesman for the world's distressed,
The champion of those who have no voices,
A leader fighting for the dispossessed,
And when they win, society rejoices.
He fights his battles with the written word
And though at times he looks to be defeated
His voice is vibrant and it will be heard
And in tense times be ardently repeated.
   The writer has a gift that he must spend:
   To rectify, to counsel and to mend.

The couplet summarizes my work ethic so far as the writer is concerned. I've hewn close to this line and have stumbled when I strayed.

-10-

When people saw that I might be a writer
A wise man gave advice profound and sane:
'I know that you by nature are a fighter
'But when the critics blast, you can't complain
'For that's their job so think of something brighter.
'Don't try riposte or struggle to explain,
'You'll not succeed, just make yourself look slighter.
'And I advise you never to disdain
'The critic, for he boasts a clout that far
'Surpasses yours: brains, style, facts and the use
'Of that huge daily paper. He's the czar
'With force to hammer you with harsh abuse.
    'You'll find recourse in only one true shot:
    'That you have writ the books and he has not.'

––––––––––

The old fellow said it more succinctly: 'Never complain,
never explain, never disdain.'

-11-

The other day I set our house on fire
While I was working in another room.
The consequences could have been most dire—
When I rushed in, it seemed a day of doom.
I'd left a small pot cooking on low flame
And it exploded with a sonic boom
With only me at hand and me to blame,
The room was soon engulfed in blaze and fume.
The pyrotechnics took my brows and hair,
Aghast I viewed the gold tempestuous blaze,
With just bare hands I slapped the raging flare
And thank the Lord! the flames died in the haze.
   My wife teased: 'You're a wonder with a book,
   'But no man born can type and also cook.'

A frightening spring day in the new Maine apartment.
Close to a total disaster.

-12-

Because my books found multitudes of readers
They gained a wealth of interesting mention
And stood quite high among best-selling leaders
While garnering much industry attention.
This brought more income than one man deserved
So I evaluated my position:
'You've preached successful writers ought to serve
'And here you are in that exact condition.'
Soulsearching led me to a bold decision:
'Because my earnings are a public treasure,
'The step that I must take is to provision
'Agencies deserving their full measure
    Of my rewards.' Obedient to these rules,
    I've given all to colleges and schools.

The obligation to spend wisely the income from my writing started early in my professional career. I never felt guilty about this problem, nor did I allow it to dominate my thinking. But it certainly determined my behavior.

-13-

Throughout my life I've been confused by money
For in my childhood there was none around.
We trusted Santa and the Easter bunny
To bring what little gifts they might have found.
So when my books sold well I was astounded
For every task I worked at turned to gold.
When wealth piled up my values were confounded
And I decided on a venture bold:
'If I began with nothing and survived it
'I'd like to exit in the self-same way.'
And when I reached my eighties I contrived it:
I gave the monies I had earned away.
    'Twas nigh a hundred million I divested
    To works of social worth that interested.

This sonnet amazes me with its frank admissions
regarding the money problems and my solution of it.

-14-

Rondeau
Of A Writer On Attaining Age
Seventy-five

I owe the world a debt of grace,
Some rental on the precious space
I am allowed to occupy
From whence I publish forth my cry
That magnifies the human race.

I never sought fame's harsh embrace.
I could depart without a trace.
The world owes me no laurels high...
   I owe the world.

So I would deem it no disgrace
Should fate determine to erase
All I have done and nullify
My passioned books, letting them die.
The world owes me no special place...
   I owe the world.

———

First published in *Testimony* in 1983.

-15-

Sonnet

To A

Weathered Wanderer

The day came when he roamed our roads no more,
His heart was willing but his strength declined.
His walking stick stood dusty by the door,
And neighbors wondered: 'Could it be his mind?'
They sent me to inquire and he explained:
'To travel far I was ordained at birth.
'So do not grieve that now I am enchained,
'The soul that soars cannot be bound to earth.
'Proust though in bed roamed Paris day and night,
'While in his garret Chatterton hatched schemes.
'Blind Milton still saw vistas of delight,
'And Emily fled Amherst in her dreams.
  'A mind can tour the world at little cost,
  'And visions once perceived are never lost.'

First published in *Literary Reflections* in 1993.

-16-

Verses To A Writer
Heading For Ninety

We see him in the twilight and the setting of the sun,
Hiking by to greet us when our working day is done.
Leaving his garden where squirrels come for food,
He walks our tree-lined paths
And climbs our little hills,
The dogs greet him with fond solicitude.

Night after night in rain or sultry heat
He makes his way along our quiet street
And throws a cheery smile
To those by chance he meets.

My little sister used to watch
Each night to see him pass
And wondered why he strode along our road:
'Have you no bed to go to when
'The stars tell us to sleep?'

He smiled at her and smoothed her hair:
'I climb the hills to give my heart
'A task to make it work
'So that I sleep at night and rise
'Again at dawn once more to strive
'At deeds I dare not shirk.'
'Did you have fun today?' she asked
And he said 'I enjoy each day
'And what it cares
'To bring my way.
'The rain or storm or starlit nights,
'I love them all.'

I sought the secret of this wandering man
And spied upon him as he passed our way,
But when I questioned him he had no plan,
And seemed content with any random day.
   'At night I see your light
   'When you get up to write
   'Why do you work so hard?'
And he replied: 'I have a double goal.
 'I work so hard to exercise my heart,
 'I write so much to activate my soul.'

   He huffed and he hobbled
   On paths that were cobbled
Till I was afraid he might fall.
   But he was defended
   By those he'd befriended
And he wasn't worried at all.

Three runners stopped beside him
   Before they passed him by:
'Why do you come to test this track
'Old man? You'll wrench your back!'
   He smiled: 'If you keep running
   'As you do these tranquil nights,
'Perhaps you'll have the strength as I
'To thus your ninety years defy.'

Young people came to talk with him
   From India and Spain,
And when they left they lugged their bags
   Of books with lighter air.

It seemed these youths his steps would vitalize.
'When you are old like me you spend your nights
'In wondering from where new talents will arise
'To dream new dreams and serve as acolytes
   'To take your place
   'When you have left.
  'Much work remains for dedicated hands
   'And searching minds.
 'The world cries out for leadership
   'Whom will it find?'

'Is that the reason you are out at night,
'Searching the streets to find a lad of worth
'To take your place?' And he said: 'No.
   'I come to watch the fading light
   'Of day that warmed the earth
'To hear the singing of the twilight birds
'To see gold shadows on the moon's pale face.
      'For if the world stays right
'Young men and women blessed with thoughts like mine
   'Will rise to sing the songs and write the books
'And feed the squirrels too when I am gone.'

      And then he sang this song:
      'O Earth, how fortunate I am
   'To have plumbed your secrets in fullest measure
'And known so well your glorious treasure
         'Your burning sands
         'Your coraled strands
         'Your turbulent seas
         'Your verdant leas
   'Volcanos with their molten fire
   'Fulfillment of the heart's desire.
'An open road with light in distant dark,
   'And strength to travel it when young
   'And memories when youth is sprung.

'That's why I walk these cobbled paths
      so patiently each night,
'A man who searches steadfastly
      will sometimes find the light.'

_____

First published in *Literary Reflections* in 1993.

-17-

The icy claw of Death clamped on my shoulder.
A mocking voice said: 'You have been so brave
'In daring Life, how will you now behave?
'The time has come, greybeard, you'll grow no older.'
And as he spoke the wind grew dark and colder,
For he was leading down into a cave.
He picked a fetid spot: 'Behold your grave
'In which in darkness you'll decay and molder.'

But through the brooding shadows thrust a light
That filled the cave and cast a golden gleam
Enfolding gloom with colors gay and bright
But ending in a solitary beam
That lured me upward, and my soul took flight
But left my books fulfillment of my dream.

I am a great devotee of the purist Petrarchian sonnet
which requires only four rhymes, two for the octet, two
for the sestet. Italian, with its plethora of liquid vowel
endings, makes the Petrarchian sonnet in that
language an easy task. In rougher, more brutal
English it becomes almost impossible. I'm proud of
this one. The eruption of death as a subject surprises
me for it is not typical of my thinking.

A headstrong little terror

-18-

In 1906 abortion was no option,
She had to take her pregnancy to term.
Nor were there systems for a quick adoption,
The laws were harsh and punishing and firm.
A mere fourteen, she wept: 'I'll keep my child,
'Without a husband, confidant or mate.'
They warned: 'What you propose is rash and wild,
'An orphanage is what we advocate.'
She would not listen. All she'd say was 'Maybe'
And she awaited birth with surging joy.
At last she held her deeply cherished baby:
A laughing, robust, nine-pound gurgling boy....
    She found for motherhood she'd no vocation
    So left him in a New York trolley station.

The only authority I have for the last line of this sonnet is
a cryptic comment I heard Uncle Arthur make one day.
He offered no further explanation, so it could have been
one of his jokes. But he said it, in my hearing.

-19-

Who was this child who acted as my mother?
I've never known though there's been speculation
And theories, one looser than the other.
We were together for a short duration
But in that time she showed me true affection,
Gave me strong genes and started me aright,
Bequeathed to me no inbred imperfection.
So though I started in a sorry plight,
I started also with her stormy will:
'I'll not surrender him, he is my child.'
She struggled on, this inept juvenile,
Confused she wept yet bravely laughed and smiled.
  But she was soon submerged in misery
  And at fifteen had to abandon me.

-20-

We never had a man about our quarters.
I had no chance for masculine attention.
Three sisters cared for me, benign supporters,
But with grave gaps we did not care to mention.
There were no fishing trips on nearby streams,
No playing catch behind the livery stable,
No manly coaching of athletic dreams,
I crept along as fast as I was able.
But when I looked about and saw how others
Were treated in a father's drunken rage,
Wives thrashed, girls raped and badly beaten brothers,
I ceased to yearn for natural parentage.
   We did not grieve for things we were denied
    But built strong lives with what fate did provide.

The song of rejection, one of my abiding character traits.
If I couldn't have it, I didn't want it.

-21-

It just occurred to me why I have wandered
So constantly throughout my scattered life:
When young we lacked a penny to be squandered,
Existence was a never-ending strife.
We scuttled back and forth through eight small shelters
Each somehow more repugnant than the other
With bugs and rats and lice all helter skelter—
Great burdens always falling on my mother.
Our home was not a gardened place to cling to
But more a spot I tried hard to avoid.
'Twas not a hallowed memory to spring to
But rather dulling, aching, cheerless void.
   I did not seek like Parsifal the summit
   Nor did I run *to* something, I ran *from* it.

A photographic record was recently made of the eight houses. One had disappeared.

I could not draw. The teacher said of me:
'This child is wasting time here in this class.'
But then I found Benozzo Gozzoli
And in one leap outdistanced fail-and-pass.
In wandering years that followed I would see
Each major art museum in the world.
Velásquez, Giotto were old friends to me,
Monet, Manet and Klee around me swirled.
I could not draw or pass the third-grade test
Or memorize the name-lists and the rules,
But I could make collections of the best
I could afford, and pass them on to schools.
    Hokusai and Ando taught me how to see,
    Piero and bold Pollock set me free.

BENOZZO GOZZOLI (1420-1497) was a Florentine painter of the second category. A pupil of Fra Angelico, he was a brilliant colorist, portraitist, and creator of multi-part murals depicting Biblical biographies. PIERO DELLA FRANCESCA (c1420-1492) was a superlative painter in new Renaissance styles, author of treatises on perspective, and creator of both vast murals and smaller easel works, including portraits of leading political figures of his day. HOKUSAI, pronounced Hoke-sai (1760-1849) was a prolific Japanese woodblock artist, famous in Europe for his wonderful series of thirty-six views of Mount Fuji, and for his *Manga*, a series of booklets containing hundreds of drawings. I published a monograph on Hokusai, one of my heroes. ANDO HIROSHIGE (1797-1858), a prolific Japanese woodblock artist, was often thought of as a twin to Hokusai. His set of prints depicting the fifty-three stages of the Tokaido, the colorful route from Tokyo (Edo in those days) to Kyoto, enjoyed a wild success. Scholars have published handsome studies of the Michener collection of Hiroshiges, several thousand in number and now residing in the Honolulu Academy of Art.

-23-

In playing games I had a modest talent,
So in the best American tradition
I fancied me a whiz. A bold gallant!
Self accolades I deemed my just commission.
We won twelve games for every one we dropped
And were the winners of our little section,
I was convinced that we could not be stopped
And told myself that we were near perfection.
In retrospect how puny was our playing!
Real stars today would run us down roughshod.
Comparison with them is quite dismaying,
Today my skill would never make the squad.
   But in the wondrous make-believe of youth
   I saw myself a star. So much for truth!

Crash the cymbals, blare the trumpets,
Wreathe their noble brows with laurel.
Heap the festive board with crumpets
And with decorations floral.
They deserve the fairest lilies—
   Who? The Phillies.

Through the long dark years they stumbled
Scarred the deep humiliations
But our cheering never crumbled
And we kept our expectations.
Yes, we loved them for their sillies—
   Who? The Phillies.

Triple plays that did not triple,
Strikeouts with the bases loaded,
Pitchers serving up the cripple,
All our hopes again exploded.
Are they not a bunch of dillies?
    Who? The Phillies.

Far behind in early innings,
Doomed to tragedy eternal,
They turn losses into winnings
Through some holy fire internal.
They give enemies the willies—
    Who? The Phillies.

Bang the drum and toot the oboes,
Dance until the earth has shaken.
Cheer, for our beloved hoboes
Have at last brought home the bacon.

Garland them with timeless lilies!
Although they are a bunch of dillies
Who give honest men the willies.
We still love them for their sillies.
    Hail, The Phillies.

When they launched their quest in the playoffs, the Phillies, always a team of infinite class, asked the city's revered musician, Eugene Ormandy, to throw out the ball for the first game, and a local scribbler to start the second.

Ormandy won his game, I lost mine, proving that the piccolo is mightier than the Smith-Corona. The flawless artistry displayed by the Phils in the series was due in large part to this graceful beginning.

While flying to Bangkok during the World Series, I was prompted to scribble a verse on hearing the pilot announce, 'The Phillies won the World Series!'

-25-

When young I was a headstrong little terror,
Did things that should have thrown me into jail.
I don't mean normal pranks and youthful error
But crimes that scar a lifetime and derail.
Then they discovered I excelled at ball games,
At math and science too and English grammar.
So soon I was in quest of gaining high aims,
Lawful pursuits that kept me from the 'slammer.'
In adult years I rendered three offenses,
Not legal crimes or torts but something worse:
Assaults against our deepest moral senses,
They haunt me as a never-ending curse.
　　Each man has pages of his life he'd blot,
　　Or episodes he blithly has forgot.

-26-

I knew why bears and beavers hibernate
And how the Roman Empire lived and died,
I knew how chromosomes decide our fate
And how the moon looks on the unseen side.
I thought that I was fairly bright, but now
Lucinda smiled at me and my head twirled,
Try as I might I could not figure how
She had acquired the wisdom of the world.
She knew just when to laugh, or pout, or purr,
To rule our school became her clear intent.
She made us boys feel bigger than we were
So we elected her class president.
   Though four score plus, I still don't have a clue
   To how young girls obtain the lore they do.

-27-

The year that we hid out on Barbo Street
My bedroom scanned the jeweler's house next door
So I observed a courtship calm and sweet,
Sam twenty-nine, and Bessie thirty-four.
Three times a week Sam ate at her expense
And never took her to a dining place,
I said: 'Such wooing really makes no sense
'He's eaten free five years, a damned disgrace.'
That August Sam was called to Army camp,
A gun misfired and put him into bed.
His men warned: 'Sam, your nurse is on the vamp!'
And at the end of August they were wed.
   But Bess was not deserted, not at all,
   Clerk Tom began free dinners late that fall.

In my teens I watched at close quarters the progress of
two country love affairs, and they had a powerful effect.
This one was comic.

-28-

When we lived briefly in the heart of town
I had a chance to study those respected:
I watched the banker with his solemn frown
And wondered: 'Why's that rich man so dejected?'
He had a daughter tall and stiff like him
Except she had this horrid upper lip
That never closed but stayed an ugly grin
As if the gods had made a thoughtless slip.
When she was twenty-eight a Don Juan came,
Seduced her for the sport, and then he left
Her pregnant and abandoned with the shame
And marked forever with both babe and cleft.
   Granpère and daughter bravely walked our street
   But tears edged forward when old friends they'd meet.

The second love affair I watched was a tragedy whose memory still brings tears.

Spring Virtue

In a nest high in the branches reaching to the sky sat a woodbird singing sadly, to the night that would not answer.

"For the emptiness of loving
Is the fullness of a death."

And the breath of an air that passed moaningly through the leaves echoed the lamentations.

For the nest, formed with care, for the eggs that once were there, now swung unused. Storms had come and the trees had bowed their heads to the lashings of the winds, and the clashing of the branches bent the nest until the four eggs fell to the earth and Death smiled upon them instead of Birth.

And the trees in the breezes that now scarcely bent or lowered heard the threnody of slumber:

"Lullaby, my unborn children,
    Lullaby.
Sleep serenely, oh my children, ·
    Sleep and rest.
For I wait here on the nest,
    Wait and weep,
With an ever watchful eye
    To guard your sleep.
    And I sigh,
A lullaby, a lullaby."

Underneath an open window sang a lover—he had come tonight to wake her from her slumbers and in hesitating numbers to tell her that he loved her.

A Summer and an Autumn and a Winter he had loved her, but the coldness of her glances and the harshness of her actions told him that his thoughts were foolish—warned him that his hopes were idle.

Now the Springtime burst upon them and the warmth of April's sunlight coupled with the birth of Maytime when all nature mates, gives and receives embraces, when flushed faces lower, blushing, having read a question, made her give an answer.

They were helpless, drunk with Springtime. Often when he passed he touched her, or her hair brushed past his face and the blood would race to his temples and to hers.

Or a shoulder strap would slide toward an elbow half revealing shoulders of a pearly whiteness, half concealing breasts of ivory.

Springtime caused these things to happen; Springtime brought him to her window with his mind filled with the visions and his aching heart articulate with song.

With a voice that faltered badly and a tune that sadly told the story he began:

> "Love, come out into the moonlight,
>   For the entire world is mating;
>   And I stand here in the starlight,
>   Waiting, waiting.
>
> Sleep has come to all but lovers
> And the night is waiting for you—
> One sad message near you hovers:
>   'I adore you.'
>
> Come, for Springtime knows no virtue,
> Spring is an eternity—
> Love, I could not harm or hurt you.
>   Do not fear me.
>
> Love, come out into the moonlight
> Where a lover waits for you.
> Swearing, in a flood of starlight:
>   'I adore you.'"

When he finished she was standing in her window, with her hair about her shoulders and a low dress banding all her loveliness.

There she stood a single moment and he caught the glimpse of beauty fraught and laden with delight—oh, the night could offer little for the Spring had brought the maiden.

But the woodbird, mourning ever for the never answered pleading sang again her song of sorrow and the trees receding in the breezes cooled the forehead of the lover as he waited for an answer:

> "Softly, gently, in the branches,
> Like a cradle swings my nest
> Empty of the eggs I gave it,
> Empty of the gifts of love.
> Oh my lullaby is ended
> Ere I sang three notes of love.
> Empty nest, like cradle rocking,
> Be my sepulchre, my tomb.
> For the emptiness of loving
> Is the fullness of a Death."

But the song of tribulation fell on ears that would not hear it, for the thought of naught but loving, and the fears and tears of nature were to him as whisperings of a question that was answered.

She was coming, Spring had called her, and the virtue of a winter faded from her as the snows melt and fade before the sun that brings the rose.

As she came he heard her singing and his answer was completed:

> "Love is like a swallow
>   As it flies
>   Through the skies,
>   Daring me to follow
> Toward a sun that blinds the eyes.

I have heard it singing
In the night.
And its flight
Is an endless winging
To an ether of delight.

Onward I must follow
Until day
Streaks the gray
And the tired sleepy swallow
Drops once more and flies away.

For my love is calling
And the moon
All too soon
From the heavens falling,
Ends the loveliness of June."

As the last words came from lips closely covered with a kiss and the freshness of her dress was crushed and crumpled in a long embrace, there came an answer from the wood-bird who had seen the lovers:

"Love is not a winging swallow
But a snake coiled round a stone.
And it lies there, cruel, hollow,
With its gay song but a moan.
Love is Death
And its breath
Chills the heart of one alone.
For my nest will hold no fledglings
And the emptiness of loving
Is the fullness of a Death."

———

Published in the Swarthmore College literary publication, *The Portfolio*, in March of 1928 when I was a lusty twenty-one.

A mystery of my intellectual life is the fact that, although I constantly wrote poetry with some of it being rather good for my age at the time, no teacher or professor or any other adult ever gave me a single word of encouragement. These sonnets can be seen, perhaps, as a very late explosion of a modest talent that long lay dormant for lack of encouragment. Had I pursued poetry during my working years, I believe I would have quickly drifted into some form of free verse. But that skill was never allowed to develop; obviously when in my 70s and 80s I returned to poetry, it was to the iambic pentameter which had become engrained in my consciousness.

Correction: Three times I was suspended from Swarthmore because of riotous behavior, and the third time might have been an expulsion had not Robert E. Spiller, head of the English Department, said in my defense: 'No young man can be all bad if he submits his term paper in iambic pentameters.' When the Dean asked: 'Were they any good?' Spiller is supposed to have said: 'Passing grade,' and my entire career was saved.

Great music filled the
crannies of my soul

-30-

How sweet the music was that filled our dwelling!
Caruso, Galli-Curci and their legion,
With Uncle Robert shouting: 'Stop that yelling!'
And Laura's sharp: 'Go to another region!'
The singers whom the world revered as kings
Were like good friends who traipsed in every day,
The stories of their operas were the wings
Which carried us to dreamlands far away.
Then came the great orchestral revelations.
Beethoven, Schubert, Brahms and gifted others
Performed for us the best of their creations.
Stravinsky, Mozart, Haydn were my brothers.
   Great music filled the crannies of my soul
   To echo there and in time make me whole.

Few amateurs have been as captive to great music as I.
The following sonnets depict that subservience.

31

I hear two women sing and it is magic,
The way their voices blend in harmony
Descanting tales both harrowing and tragic:
Norma, Lakme, Butterfly are three.
I hear two men in passages of power:
Don Carlo, Pearl Fishers and *Othello,*
I hear the solemn pledge of the avower
In passages that vibrate like a cello.
And when I hear a tenor and soprano
Their voices blazing themes of love and passion:
Mimi, Rhadames and Cio-cio-san in throe,
Doomed lovers, my heart trembles with compassion.
  'Tis nature's law: the purest harmony
    Relies upon the motif 'She-and-He.'

32

Caruso sang for me again last night
From out a disk graved eighty years ago,
A tenor prone to bold bravissimo.
His voice was reedy, hesitant and slow,
Unable now to reach that soaring height
That used to give the world such keen delight.

I blamed it on my faulty audio
That dulled a voice with once tremendous bite
And magnified each scratched adagio.

But when he reached the aria *M'Appari*
His voice rose to a majesty sublime
And every blemish vanished in high C.

I gasped at golden musical perfection
And heard why he had claimed the world's affection.

-33-

My task is words but loved with passion deep
The Philadelphia with its stern control,
The glory of its brass, the syncopated roll
Of kettle drums, the tuba's brazen brays,
Kincaid the flautist, and suave Tabateau
Whose oboe's notes created sweet bouquets,
The french horns with their rich autumnal show.
King of them all, Stokowski and his mane
Of snow-white hair and daring new transcriptions
Of Bach and other works o'er which he reign'd—
Great music played with powerful convictions.
   The Philadelphia taught me how to listen
   And comprehend their art form's grand tradition.

-34-

Our songbird with the golden smile and voice
Sang us the songs we loved: *Rainbow, Beguine*
And *Trolley Car.* To hear them we rejoiced:
'Brava! Encore!' We made a noisy scene.
Our cheers rang out as we heard *Smokey Eyes*
And *Just Plain Bill* and *Man That Got Away*
And *Love for Sale.* They really took the prize
And we'd have stayed until the break of day.

We hushed for throaty, sweet accented words:
La Vie en Rose, Milord and *No Regrets*
And *Village in the Vale* with golden chords
That seemed to come from angel-like duets.
Our vast hall stilled in silent adoration
Of 'Little Sparrow,' darling of her nation.

———

At sea off the Aleutians, October 7, 1993

*To watch this flow of
life has been most
thrilling*

-35-

I knew a girl, a lovely Indian miss
Who came to town a stranger in our school.
We fell in love, she pledged it with a kiss
And I rejoiced: 'I am a lucky fool!'
But then her brother, dark of eye and mien,
Grabbed at my throat and warned that he would kill
If on their farm I evermore was seen....
I fled and left her though I loved her still.
His was not idle threat. He had a plan
For sudden wealth. He mobilized a gang
But things went sorely wrong. They killed a man
And on a rain-swept day we saw him hang.
   She fled our town, not stopping for goodbyes,
   Her craven lover left with endless sighs.

When I finally discovered girls, the effect was cataclysmic,
intertwined with murder.

-36-

Our village had a girl of classic grace,
A form divine and skilled in all the arts.
She had a haughty mien, a graven face,
But when she smiled she broke a dozen hearts.
Her parents taught that she was far above
Her suitors of our ordinary breed.
They warned her 'Don't be tricked by easy love,
'A knight is waiting on a snow-white steed.'
The years passed and her champion never came,
We begged her: 'Choose your lover from this town!'
But she stood firm. Her answer was the same:
'I'm destined for a man of great renown.'
    The seven who loved her bore her up the hill
    And buried her, and she is waiting still.

This sonnet is a tribute to a splendid girl whose life is
accurately described, but like the line in Sonnet 4 it is
also a deferential nod to Robert Browning's *A
Grammarian's Funeral.* I cherish the four lines which
define what the great man accomplished:

> He settled *Hoti's* business—let it Be!—
>   Properly based *Oun*—
> Gave us the doctorine of the enclitic *De*,
>   Dead from the waist down.

-37-

With seven seconds left he kicked a goal
And won the playoffs, thirty/thirty-three.
Within five minutes cars were on the roll
To shatter sable night with revelry.
They torched a row of stores and looted others,
When ambulances came they sent them flying
Roofs ablaze. A medic shouted: 'Brothers!
'We're here to save the wounded and the dying!'
Where'er the hero went he met applause
For his field goal had won for them the game,
So when he heard the shouting without pause
The thought came: 'Yes, I do deserve this fame.'
  The other score: three dead, and wounded eighty-six,
  The night he won the playoff with his kicks.

-38-

Tim Clancy was our archetypal stud,
No girl could look at him without complying.
Compared to him I was a total dud
So pitiful I almost stopped applying.
Each night he showed up with a different maiden
And he was taking most of them to bed,
Sex was his sport. He never was guilt-laden.
He guzzled too and gambled so we said
That he'd die broke from wild and reckless betting.
Not so. We others took Bankrupt Eleven
While with wife six Tim reveled in jet-setting
And wound up in financial seventh heaven.
  When first I learned these facts they seemed amusing
  But I'm a moralist and they're confusing.

There was no keener scholar in our school,
A polymath before that word was known.
He knew of computations, laws, the rule
Of three-four-five, the volume of the cone.
He led a brilliant life. Our village cheered
As he received the world's profound applause
And accolades for having engineered
Solutions to some strange perplexing flaws.

In one great field he failed, the human heart.
He could not see that love had problems vaster
Than could be solved by diagnostic chart.
So thrice a marriage ended in disaster
Because he never learned that life's an art
And love a force booklearning cannot master.

-40-

He was the cynic in our seminar,
A man who laughed at any perceived fact
With ridicule that left an aching scar.
He had no sense of tenderness or tact
And sneered at men like me of gentler mood.
His theme on Milton showed his savage wit
For it contained a line obscene and crude:
'So Lycidas is dead? Who gives a ****?'
They wanted to expel him, but I pled:
'We need his sharp attack, his snide foray,
'Through his keen eyes we see the way ahead.'
And with my help he was allowed to stay.
    I'd learned that concepts cynics forge in youth
    Are often closest to the timeless truth.

Vulgar epithet in four letters.

She was my leading lady on the stage
In three grand dramas she became my bride.
Her art expanded, she became the rage,
I could not cope and had to step aside.
But yet I followed every move she made
Until her flaming comet left the skies.
She quit the stage and I was sore dismayed
To watch her settle for the lesser prize
Of teaching novices and taking tasks
That must have been degrading to her pride.
But proudly still she wore the stage's masks:
Tragic and Comic, and I could not chide.
   O radiant star! You did betray your art
   But scintillated ever in my heart.

The three stage plays were *Twelfth Night* by William
Shakespeare, 1601, *Outward Bound* by Sutton Vane,
1923, and *Skidding* by Aurania Rouverol of Pocatello,
Idaho, 1928. This last play, featuring Judge Hardy and
his rambunctious son Andy, became the base for the
wildly popular Andy Hardy series of motion pictures. My
role was quickly dropped and my co-star's role was
submerged and then given to young Judy Garland,
whence the immortal line: 'Hey, Kids! Let's do a play in
the barn!'

-42-

In the Old Hebrides I knew a lass
The soul of Gaelic Scotland, for her songs
Embraced the elfin echoes of the past
And chronicled the mournful ancient wrongs.
In ceilidh soft we sang till break of day
The Hebridean *Lilt of Eriskay.*

In the New Hebrides I knew a dame
From Indo-China living in a hut.
Who could have dreamed that I would bring her fame,
Her toothful grin bestained with betel nut?
But she was tough. We formed a doughty pair
And bent the war our way to grab our share.

How fortunate at any stage of life
To find such women to be spirit-wife!

––––––––

Ceilidh (kay-lee) is the language of a midnight Gaelic
songfest around a peat fire.

-43-

Daughter of Fuji and the old Japan
Girl of tatami and the sliding door,
I am the soul-exhausted fighting man
Who came to know you at the end of war.
You preached that peace was now the only course
And took me to Hakone seeking art,
You said our nations must surrender force
But much, much more, you gave me of your heart.
You will not see this proof of my affection
For it remains a secret till I die,
But I shall give my ghost a firm direction:
'Take up my poem, cherish it, and hie
'Thee to Japan, my enemy of yore,
'And fix this gift of love upon her door.'

-44-

She was quite brave, this child of alien race
Who dared to be my loyal, loving wife.
She showed abundant and unwavering grace
In battling the vicissitudes of life.
Thrown into prison at the start of war,
She never cursed her fate or placed a blame
Or schemed to settle some ignoble score,
Grim tribulations cruel she overcame.
Her stubborn conscience and her searching mind
Are dedicated to a world in peace.
Her attributes she shares with all mankind
I watch with pride as her good deeds increase.
   How fortunate our lives were intertwined,
   She is the gem that I was blest to find.

———————

It must be obvious by now that I see the contemporary
sonnet as an offering of fourteen lines whose rhyme
scheme can alter wildly. I like that freedom and have used
it vigorously. In this sonnet one sound—mind, mankind,
intertwined, find—dominates in a manner that no classi-
cist would have tolerated. I think it works.

-45-

How to describe my lovely laughing mate?
Her face is like a shining harvest moon
Stippled with gold. Dark eyes illuminate
All that she does. Her radiant smiles bestrewn
Among her friends reap cheerfulness and joys.
Her zest is real, not fashioned for occasion,
Infectious, so my sloth is fast destroyed.
A forthright soul not given to evasion,
Her heart brims high with love. She knows devotion
And longs to share it with another being
If he can but reciprocate emotion
And recognize in life what is worth seeing.
   Much blessed, I found this woman for my wife
   And learned the true significance of life.

————————

This sonnet, written in 1972, was read by the Presbyterian minister, a woman, at Mari Michener's funeral service in Austin at the end of September 1994.

Bound in gallant brotherhood together

46

Halacious storm clouds hemmed my island station,
So every time that I was called to duty
In our small plane we faced thick deadly beauty
And fought to make a twisting penetration.
We'd drop a thousand terrifying feet
Then fly two minutes with our plane inverted
And fight like hell to get the thing reverted
For aerobatic aerial repeats.
In brawls with storms our plane was strong but crude:
The DC-3, workhorse of aviation.
In each affray it won our adulation
As we broke free to peaceful solitude.
   Those who survived that dark and hellish weather
   Were bound in gallant brotherhood together.

I flew this semi-permanent tropical front several dozen
times and was always terrified.

47

How many times I left my duty spot
And flew out to the shifting battle zone
To cruise the many islands in *The Slot*
Which we were slowly taking as our own.
Iron Bottom Bay lay shimmering below
Where rusting ships lay sunken by the score,
The pilots dropped down very low to show
Us where some great ship rusted on the shore.
But always when our recon safely ended
We faced the dreadful flight back to the start,
Where hid a front incessantly suspended
With turbulence to tear a plane apart.
   We'd drop a thousand feet and see waves breaking
   Then leap two thousand with our bodies shaking.

The Slot is a line well traveled by war planes flying from
Guadalcanal to Bougainville and vice versa.

-48-

At half past one I joined a small patrol,
A leader and eight men, to find the site
On which the foes were bivouacked that night,
Our men maintaining disciplined control.
As we crept ever closer to our goal
Abruptly flamed a blaze of flashing light
And we were threatened with a deadly fight
But we stayed closely knit and came out whole.
The man beside me was a lad from Macon
Still in his teens and shaking with emotion
But very proud: 'We're bringing home the bacon!'
It was just then we took a vast explosion.
　At G.H.Q. I helped to draft the wire:
　'The cause of death: Incoming friendly fire.'

─────────

A midnight incident in the Korean mountains.

-49-

Because the airline pilots loved my books
They frequently invited me to share
Their view, so I could see how nature looks
When seen from the exalted upper air.
They said: 'We do not wish to be misleading.
'It's not your art that helps us through the nights
'But that your books are huge with ample reading
'To help us pass our often boring flights.'
Once in Brazil the pilots came to greet me:
'Today we fly the length of our great river.
'Ride with us in the cockpit, you will then see
'Much better. Here's a sight for any writer.'
   On earth no more sublime phenomenon:
   Blue sky above, below green Amazon.

-50-

Another time at midnight pilots said:
'We fly tonight the grand reach of the ocean
'Your tomes have treated with such great devotion,
'Bejeweled with isles your books have heralded.

'Fly as co-pilot. You will see below
'A world that only terns and eagles know.'

There in the magic darkness Tonga shone,
Bold Fiji with its multitude of isles
Plus chains of coral reefs with names unknown
And then the blest Hawaii, land of smiles.

As dawn broke in the east, the noble sight
Of Diamond Head, Oahu's guardian post,
A sight spent travelers have treasured most,
The culmination of a mystic flight.

One of a score of such night flights, this one from New
Zealand to Hawaii.

-51-

Three times my plane crashed in the far Pacific,
Thrice I escaped with only modest danger.
These crack-ups in the sea were not horrific
Because I knew that I was not a stranger
But an old hand returning to my ocean
About which I had written with affection.
And so I felt, without undue emotion
That it should succor me who sought protection.
Each time I left the waters aquiline
To seek another flight toward destination.
As soon as possible I strapped back in
To search the air and sea, my avocation.
  I find elation in a ship or plane,
    Always prepared to venture forth again.

––––––––––

The last line expresses my credo.

-52-

I made the broad Pacific second home,
Each distant isle a portion of my being.
I studied as its curling, twisting foam
Revealed a thousand incidents worth seeing.
The blazing sun upon the coral strand
The multitude of stars on high at night
The lonely atoll with its golden sand
The solitary bird in stately flight.
But most of all that special breed of people
Bronzed in the sun and marked by endless laughter,
Clustered about their sacred coral steeple,
Untainted by the fear of hell hereafter.
   They were the crowning joy of island life,
   Born without envy, bitterness or strife.

-53-

I sailed a small boat back across the ocean.
We had been promised it would be a trip
Of sheer delight: 'A gentle sea-wave motion
As if in crossing on a larger ship.'
But first day out the winds began to howl,
Propelling waves up to titanic height.
The timbers strained, complaining with deep growl
When thrust into the hurricane that night.
I took the wheel. They lashed me to the mast,
And waves came crashing down into my face.
The boat careened. I feared it could not last
But then it righted and survived the pace.
   Pitch-black the night, I standing all alone,
   Then to the east a break where sunlight shone.

Bucking a hurricane from Hawaii to San Francisco.

-54-

How strange, how odd, how far beyond prediction
That I should serve as NASA academe.
My work had been within the field of fiction,
Now I was tasked to join that brilliant team
To guard our nation's pathway to the moon.
How fine the men I worked with, how devoted
To keeping monstrous instruments in tune
To do the task for which they were promoted.
Those who conducted missions were mere mortals
But of heroic character and breed.
They carried courage to the outer portals
We ordinary humans rarely need.
   I watched them work and saw unearthly beauty,
   To write of them became a moral duty.

———————

Out of the blue I was shifted from Naval Aviation to
NASA's exploration of space.

-55-

Before my NASA service I knew space,
Our galaxy I'd learned about in books.
Each planet I could put in rightful place
And stars I could determine by their looks.
I worked on every process simulator
And studied manuals for prolonged flight,
Then summarized the human explicator
Required before the rockets could ignite.
But best of all I studied every minute
Of my imagined flight of exploration
To see the moon's dark side and what was on it—
The Russians knew but we lacked information.
  In time I knew each second of that mission
  And I flew upward with my erudition.

I served in NASA posts around the world but never
reached Ascension Island in the South Atlantic, a gap
in my education which galls me still.

I owe the world

-56-

The open road exerted such a lure
That I was captured by the age of twelve.
My future life would constitute a tour
Of distant regions where the mind could delve
Into accomplishments of all the races,
To tramp the paths, to taste the foods, to see
The grand memorials, the hidden places,
Relics of grandeur and of majesty.
But best of all to see the moon aglow
Upon some lofty ice-bound mountain crest
Beneath which elks and moose stand in the snow
And birds go winging to their wintry nest.
   The road tempts me and keeps me moving on
   To greet the new day and the coming dawn.

-57-

That I enjoyed the road there is no question,
The novelty, the sunshine on my face,
To choose a fork at any stray suggestion
And never brood about a sleeping place.
Awake at dawn to hear birds overfly,
To feel heart skip while hiking down the road,
How grand those mountains rising to the sky!
How sweet the smell of barley fields fresh mowed!
But ever as I headed toward the west
I felt the pull of home, the call of friends,
Remembering kith and kin laid quest to rest
So like Gray's shepherd homeward I would wend.
   I could have settled anywhere on earth
   But always sought the fair land of my birth.

Our little town, Doylestown, Pennsylvania, was unique in America for having two Rhineland castles, turrets and all, one at the northeast edge of town, one at the southwest edge. Erected in the early 1900s and today distinguished museums, they were magical affairs, and I grew up with them as a major landmark of my psychological landscape.

-58-

One evening at a camp in Idaho
A gang of older bums lambasted me:
'You'll never be a hobo till you show
'That you can ride the rods like Jake and me.'
I took their dare. They led me to the yards
And showed me how to slip myself in place
Beneath the freight and how to set up guards
To keep the burning cinders from my face.
It was a trip through hell. I was not ready
For bumps and jolts and red-hot ash aplenty
And eardrums shattered by harsh rhythm steady.
They jeered: 'Go home and come back when you're twenty.'
    I crept away but Jake came to my side:
    'Take heart young sprig. Few men can take that ride.'

-59-

Largest of all the segments of the earth
Roll ever onward, great Pacific Ocean.
I once was sent to scan your entire girth
And sleep at night lulled by your timeless motion.
I met your splendid Eskimos and Maoris
And Asians bold and gentle Polynesians.
I searched your golden sands for silvered cowries,
Enchanted by the gracious Melanesians.
Three times my planes crashed in your farthest reaches
And you sustained me, gave me back my life.
For years I lingered on your dream-like beaches
And chose one of your daughters for my wife.
  Great sea! You bring my eyes and ears deep pleasure
  And animate my spirits without measure.

Written at sea off Kodiak
September 29, 1993

-60-

The poets sing of beauty, so shall I,
Of island girl with spirits undefiled
Lighthearted 'neath unsullied azure sky,
A soul to cherish, nature's guileless child.
But I would also sing the island man
Courageous far beyond the dreams of glory,
Performing mortal feats Promethean
And bringing honor to his ocean's story.
With frail canoes but bold audacity
He led his people on vast explorations,
Hawaii and New Zealand and Tahiti,
Two thousand miles with no known destinations.
  Man of the islands clothed in beauty,
  Immortal symbol of the call to duty.

-61-

The fairest island in the seven seas
Is Bora Bora in her grand lagoon,
A thousand palm trees bending in the breeze,
Arpeggios in lyric island tune.
A chain of coral gemstones rims the bay,
A necklace round the central granite core
Of a volcano from another day
A million years ago. Bestringing shore,
A host of golden children are at play,
Their beauty garland to this lovely isle
On which I served in tarnished days of war
But which I yet remember with a smile.
  An island now of beauteous happiness,
    Your peace is solace from the world's duress.

The loveliest island of all, my second home.

The island women were a gasping shock
To European sensibilities,
They would not wear the missionary smock
Or any other dress below the knees.
They loved the white man and his gallant ways
And saw no need to masquerade their passion,
Their critics were left stunned in bemused daze
As they made love in laughing island fashion.

They lived protected by revered tradition
That every babe was guaranteed a dwelling
So unwed girls could pass their child to others.
There was no savage social admonition
Nor ugly bastard words nor cruel expelling
Since older women yearned to serve as mothers.

-63-

The island day I never can forget
Came when our thoughtful sailor boy Jean-Paul
Announced that henceforth he would be Paulette.
We whisked him to the store and purchased all
That she would need to validate this change:
Soft pointed shoes, six dresses, three fine rings,
A washer-dryer, a used kitchen range
And half a dozen other girlish things.
A social leader gave a Paris sweater
And said while watching Paul mince down the street:
'I think as Paulette, Paul is doing better.
'Last night she told us something rather sweet:
  '"I tried as Paul and found no satisfaction
  '"But now I am Tahiti's main attraction."'

Twice I attended formal gatherings in which some man
announced that he would henceforth be a woman.

-64-

When I was young I was bedazed by Spain—
Her golden past five centuries away
When kings and nobles of great worth held sway
With deeds of valor to defend their reign
Against the dread invaders, horrid bane
Of Muslim hordes in powerful display.
Great was their vict'ry on that fateful day,
With many of my heroes downed and slain.

But then came peace, with Christian kings supreme.
Instead of soldiers, artists took the lead
And Spain resumed her visionary dream.
Velásquez and El Greco now were freed,
The visions of Cervantes forged the theme,
Te Deums of Vittorio hymned their creed.

    Reborn, Spain's art and words and music sang.
    Her glories great throughout my childhood rang.

––––––––––

    I was a prisoner of Spain's allurements and still am.

- *65* -

Dos Sabios
From the Spanish of Calderón

A wise man of whom oft they tell, one day
Became so poor and needy in his state,
That he could scarce sustain himself with what he ate
Of herbs, that grew along the way.
'Is there another wretch,' he paused to say,
'Upon this earth more poor, more sad than I?'
And when his head he lowered with a sigh,
A sudden answer found he, for there kneeled
Another wise man, eating from the field
Even the refuse he had thrown away.

This is the most important poem in this series, insofar as
its influence upon me is concerned. Written in high school,
it was a tribute to an exemplary teacher of Spanish, Miss
Garner, who was so understanding, helpful and encourag-
ing that I composed in her honor a series of poems trans-
lated from the Spanish. This was the best.

  She was so moved by my gesture that she wrote to her
college, Swarthmore: 'I think my student James Michener
is exactly the kind of energetic and gifted young fellow that
you seek for one of your new scholarships.' As a conse-
quence I received a four-year board-room-tuition scholar-
ship. Swarthmore thus became the first of nine colleges,
universities and centers of learning I attended, always at
public expense via scholarships and fellowships.

-66-

I lived in Spain so I could catch the flavor
Of daily life: the tapa bars with dishes
Dispensing odors that one yearned to savor
And special foods beyond my fondest wishes.
There was flamenco, too, the vivid dancing,
The midnight concerts in the small cafes
With castanets and austere macho prancing
And singing in a dozen mournful ways.

But most of all the bullfight afternoons
With gallantry and courage on parade,
The six-piece music playing taurine tunes
As matadors in costume left the shade
And marched into the blazing glare of sun
To give brave battle till the day was done.

-67-

When the immortal caravels passed through
That splendid crescent of the Carib isles,
They left the grim Atlantic, and the crew
Huzzahed to burst into a sea of smiles.
The waves were gentler here, the breezes soft,
The sun irradiated all the sea.
Bright-colored birds sang as they soared aloft
To celebrate this subtle victory.

It was strange treasure that he found this day,
Columbus of the never-bending mind:
Not gold or silver of the facile kind
Sought by his queen, who lusted for Cathay.
He found new lands of ordinary clay,
Two continents of hope for all mankind.

Published in 1989 in *Caribbean.*

-68-

I first knew Spain in days when freedom perished,
The death of everything that I had prized,
The strangulation of the goals I'd cherished,
The triumph of the things I had despised.
In those dark days I thought the world had ended
And vowed I'd see Spain's countryside no more.
But then my lasting love for her transcended
The evil days, and I came as before.
Then saw I Spain in her historic glory:
The Roman days, the years when Islam flourished.
My heart beat faster as I heard the story
Of how the continent was ruled and nourished.
  España's caravels sped o'er the ocean
  To set new hemispheres in vibrant motion.

-69-

Before us in the darkness lay the waste
Of mighty Dasht-i-Margo and its sands.
To reach Herat we had to move in haste
But driver Malik had sure head and hands:
'We'll make it, Sahib, if you know the stars.'
There was no roadway, just the endless dune
And isolated ruins, rampant scars
Of kingdoms past, lit by a fitful moon.
How meaningful to navigate all night
As the great emperors had in ages past,
And go where Alexander in his might
Had led his thousand camels all amassed.
   Ahead I saw our midnight trip was done—
   The mosques of Herat gleaming in the sun.

Dasht-i-Margo is an immense desert lying between Kandahar and Herat in Afghanistan. I traveled on it many times, occasionally at night, navigating by the stars.

70

China! You still lie sleeping in the Hall
Of History. You deem contact a sin:
Your master work of art—that mighty wall—
Locked others out but also locked you in.
The ages passed. You stayed an outlaw nation
And stopped all flow of major contribution.
You stood aloof in stubborn isolation
And paid a fearful price in dissolution.
World's social revolutions passed you by
And you escaped the orderly progression:
Free schools, great factories that reached the sky,
And freedom, still mankind's sublime possession.
  China! Rejoin the leaders of the world
  And see your flag of liberty unfurled.

71

Broad Mackenzie helped to speed us
Caribou came down to feed us
Arctic winds could not defeat us
Ravens came to guide and greet us.

Endless nights were not oppressive
For our minds flared forth in wonder
Never mean nor small-possessive
As we talked our world asunder.

Blizzards whistled in but spared us
Challenge tempted us and dared us.

Borealis explodes in the night
Leaping and twisting in tortured forms
Conflagrations of shimmering light
Heavens ablaze in celestial storms.
Arcs in the sky
Tumble and tremble
Teasing the eye
With forms they resemble.
There leaps a bridge to the moon
Here drops a chasm to hell
Soars high that silver balloon
Borealis ablaze and all's well.
Patterns tremendous
Clashes stupendous
Behold that vast fire as it rages
Then fades to pastel as it ages
And drifts from the sky all too soon
Borealis asleep and all's well.

Spring days bring cheer
No cold to fear
New sun to warm
Nothing to harm
Arctic gods sat on our shoulder
Whisp'ring to us 'Bolder, bolder!'
We became the lords of winter
Brushing off the icy splinter
Dangling from our frozen portal
Till the cry came 'You are mortal.'

––––––––

The Mackenzie, a river in northwestern Canada, fea-
tured prominently in *Journey*, in which these lyrics
were first published.

-72-

Mighty Mackenzie, enraged at our boldness,
Drew from the lakes she hid high in her mountains
Torrents of water locked up in the coldness
Sent it cascading in perilous fountains.
Ice blocks as big as an emperor's palace
Gouged out whole forests and left the trees bending
Lurking to snatch at young men unattending
Eager to drown them in hideous malice.

Described in *Journey* as 'eight unsatisfactory lines of an extended threnody in an unusual meter.'

-73 -

Hark! From the distant village tolls the bell
Summoning to prayer all those who feel the need
Of more than mortal sustenance. These rites
Can be discharged by those who hear the cry
Of brass on brass to speed the well-worn prayer,
To bless the child newborn or ease the gray
And palsied head to its eternal rest.
I hear a sterner call: the road untrod,
The heathen who has never seen the light,
The passage through dark seas uncharted still,
The desert that they claim no man can pass,
The virgin mountain peaks ne'er stepped upon,
The lure of gold still hiding in the ground,
The call, the call from some untended Grail:
'Find me! Rescue me before I tarnish!
And yours shall be the shout of triumph...'

———————

A Requiem first published in *Journey*.

...the fault was mine.
I visualized the Grail a shining light,
Perceptible from any vale in which
I and my helpers struggled. It would be
A constant beacon, milestone in the sky,
  Signalling far
  Calling to goal.
I did not comprehend that it could function
Only by flashing back light from me. Its gleam
Existed, but in partnership with mine,
And I had launched the search a blind man,
Nothing within myself to guide the way,
No silver in my soul to match the blaze
Of what I sought, nor did I test the peaks
That would forever bar me from my goal
Till I broke through with force and fortitude
To conquer them and in my victory
  Conquer myself as well.
I see my fellow seekers lost in darkness
And know that I have failed to lead the way.
Mountains engirt us, rivers swirl, we lose
Our trail and cry: 'Reluctant Paladins we,
Who seek our Golden Grail by fleeing from it.'

————

The closing lines of *Journey's* unfinished Requiem.

-75-

'Which of *your* roads are etched in memory?'
In Arctic Norway and its endless night
We lost our way, knew panic, chanced to see
The town of Tromsö bathed in blessed light.
And in Ceylon, land of narcotic dreams,
We dared alone to venture boldly forth
To watch great elephants at play in streams
While Tamils murdered strangers in the north.
Once on the fragrant isle of Upolu
I trod a path the tropic sun had kissed
And as I gazed out toward the ocean blue
Dark maidens rose like Venus through the mist.
   I treasure all the roads, despite their bends,
   That brought me to warm hearths and trusted friends.

Upolu is the capital island of Western Samoa, the home of
Robert Louis Stevenson from 1890 to 1894.

The church stands central

76

Religion is the spiritual glue
That binds the segments of a life together,
Ethic is nothing if it is not true
To ancient lore that has survived the weather
Of all the storms that beat on it in vain.
Our morals to be strong must capsulate
Truths of the Koran, Gita and the train
Of sacred books that teach and illustrate.
I love our Bible for its splendid tales
Of ancient peoples and their thirst for God.
I follow them to probe unfathomed vales
And marvel at the tortured path they trod.
  The rhythms of that Book abide in me
  And I live ever in its majesty.

77

With rugged Deuteronomy my guide
I was Old Testament in my convictions.
With stalwart Moses ever at my side
I shivered at the prophets' maledictions
And marched with Joshua in the line of battle
To signal when the enemy was near,
And crept with Judah when we raided cattle.

How sweet the Psalms of David on the ear,
How great the tale of Job, and Samson's strife,
And always sounding strong and loud and clear:
The struggle of the Jews to build their life
Obedient to God's will, a tribe apart,
Marked always by its dedicated heart.

78

I love to read in Pentateuch, the Bible's
Opening books which Hebrews call their Torah.
They illustrate how nomads who were tribal
Became a nation history holds in awe.
The verse portrays tribes armed and well equipped
For slowly gathering strength until their capture
And exile into Babylon and Egypt
Without loss of their fierce religious rapture.
Throughout the Testament we see the Jews
Do battle with the Lord, a race defiant,
And we must ask: 'Why ever did God choose
'A group that was so brash and self-reliant?'
    God treasures courage and determination
    So He Himself ordained the Jewish nation.

79

I have observed the evils that can flow
From Revelations, strangest in the tome.
Its readers grow distraught as visions grow,
They seek the cipher of that catacomb.
Caught in this frenzy they accept the doom
Of earth and cataclysmic mad destruction,
Attempting to escape its ominous gloom,
They try obedience to its seer instructions.
Homes, children, wives and wealth all are forsaken
As they accept its agitated preaching.
When sanity is lost or badly shaken,
They try reliance on its cryptic teaching.
  Apocalyptic visions dull the senses
   Til one cannot foresee the consequences.

-80-

He is a man whom readers can adore,
The Gospels bring him agelessly alive
With gentleness and love ne'er known before
But tempered with determined need to strive
To build a new world with a kinder face.
He preached the end of war, the start of peace,
The love of children and the warm embrace
Of brotherhood. He warned men to release
Their slaves, attend the poor, and share their wealth.
He helped the widow and restored the sick
And brought the dying back to robust health.
He used the parable, not vain rhetoric.
   Disciples called him Christ the Lord but He
   Moved with the people in humility.

No one can presume to deal with moral values in the life of individuals or societies without coming face to face with the towering figure of Jesus Christ. Much of the goodness in life stems from his guidance, to which I submit. I am less impressed with theology or sponsorship of a specific religion. This nest of sonnets bespeaks my fascination with this problem and my sometimes confusion.

His life on earth was filled with work and wonder.
Born in a manger home to lowing cattle,
His work would tear the world he knew asunder
And lead to never-ending strife and battle
Between old wisdom and the new he preached.
He was a rabbi steeped in old tradition
And so he taught, until the point was reached
When mankind learned a wholly new submission
To the will of God and found salvation.
How kind he was, how gentle in his manner,
Enfolding all the world as congregation—
Earth's peoples bound as one under his banner.
   Christ Jesus was a man without compare
   His kind, redeeming love lives everywhere.

-82-

How can a man revered as Prince of Peace
Become the cause of brutal wars unending—
Theistic skirmishes that never cease?
Where'er I look I see this constant rending!
Muslim and Jew in Holy Land unknit,
Muslim and Christian in a score of places,
Each side condemning other counterfeit
And citing scripture as the warring basis.
Catholic and Catholic contest forlorn Croatia,
Christians kill in northern Ireland,
Muslim and Christian draw their swords in Asia,
Fight vicious wars to gain the upper hand.
   Crusade! Jihad! Fierce bugle calls to action
   Demanding triumph of *their* true faith's faction.

-83-

The only time I dared accept the Host
At any Roman Mass that I attended
Was from the priest whom I respected most:
The Polish cardinal I had befriended,
Jan Pavel Drugi, now John Paul the Second.
And when he passed the sacred wafer to me
It was as if the Christ Himself had beckoned
And we were on the shore at Galilee.
In that brief moment I perceived the power
Of this frail man who can admonish nations
And chastize evil trying to devour
His faithful world-wide flock of congregations.
   How strange for me, a rural silent Quaker
   To share the morning with this great earth-shaker.

Struck off at four in the morning while lying in bed, but
I'd been thinking of the subject for some time.

-84-

Deep in the woods I heard an ancient gong
Invoking monks to prayer in their old shrine,
And as they passed me by in saffroned throng
I heard a slack-jawed half-wit's crooning chime:
'Ta-reem, Ta-ram, Ta-room, Ta-rilee-ree.'
The monks ignored his mad foolhardihood,
But when the parade's fool came up to me
He smiled gap-toothed as if I understood.
Then from the temple came a god-like chorus:
And radiance divine surrounded me:
'List to the foolish one. His words speak for us,
'La-reem, La-ram, La-room, La-lilee-lee!'
   If gods speak to the world in arcane jumbles
   Will they not understand the idiot's mumbles?

At sea off Japan, October 8,1993

-85-

In Bamian the Buddha smiled at me
Ineffable, inscrutable, serene.
From this grand Vale he altered history
And made East Asia his ordained demesne.
His was a peaceful truth. If I'm correct
He never led his acolytes in war,
Preferring to devise and then perfect
His teachings for a world superior.
China, Korea and aloof Japan
Surrendered to his gentle admonitions
Regarding the desired aspects of man
And his immortal after-life transitions.
  He gave another proof of his great heart:
  Where'er his people went they left fine art.

Bamian is a vale of stately grace west of Kabul. It is
sacred to Buddhism for through it this religion was
disseminated to Eastern Asia.

Beijing,
October 16, 1993

-86-

I cannot understand how churches falter
Since Christ ordained and sent them on their way.
How can they willfully profane their altar
And flagrantly transgress and disobey?
Swaggert cajoled and Bakker feigned a sham,
Their antics ridiculed our sacred Father
With scandalous sins against the Holy Lamb.
One wonders why our pious people bother
With such crazed fools. But there was worse to come:
Guyana's Jones and Waco's mad Koresh
Committed crimes so foul the nation trembled.
With psychic force their converts were enmeshed
And met their fates in grisly deaths assembled.
   I laud the church, the good it introduces
   But loath weird preachers it ofttimes produces.

-87-

I would not care to live in any town
That had no church to even evil's score,
For churches bring distinction and renown
And dignity and brotherhood and more:
Here boys and girls can meet, and some years later
Mold marriages ordained to work and last,
Church friendships are young people's integrator,
Advantages of membership are vast.
The church stands central like a timeless pillar
Supporting all the burden of its missions,
Its ardent dream: to worship the Creator
As stately guardian of mankind's traditions.
  Happy the town that has dynamic churches
  Sorry the town whose citizenry still searches.

*Simple truths that
reign eternally*

-88-

Rondeau
Of A Compulsive Worker
On His Eightieth Birthday

Full eighty times the cock has crowed
Not for the day but for the year,
Shouting his admonition clear:
'Awake! The testing time is near
And you must reap the crop you sowed.'

Each dawn I left my warm abode
And worked till every sheaf was stowed,
Then checked to see the field was clear
    Full eighty times.

And as I sweated by the road,
Apologetic for the code
That drove me so, I chanced to hear
God's voice: 'I shall not interfere,
But you toil in a field I hoed
    Full eighty times.'

First printed in 1983 in *Testimony*, then reprinted
in 1993 in *Literary Reflections*. I am deeply moved
by the last stanza as I read it at age eighty-nine.

89

A nation's ethic is the group of rules
That govern tests of ordinary life:
A city must provide the best of schools
A husband must protect his kids and wife
A man must go a full mile and beyond
Employers do deserve eight hours sweat
A handshake must be treated like a bond
And men are honor bound to pay a debt.
Much of this rural wisdom comes from games:
Both teams deserve a level playing field.
And in each game there is a last resort:
A wrong decision still can be appealed.
   It's true that men will fight for golden rings
   But rules of ethics limit ravagings.

90

A man who lives obedient to his ethic
Slowly earns a proud and honored name,
His work may not be highly praised or epic
But friends award him quiet local fame.
He rears his childen, none of them in jail,
He helps his wife become a stalwart matron
Who serves her obligations without fail,
For every worthy cause he is a patron.
Is this a modern life that's worth the living?
Subservient ever to a set of rules?
Taking so little but so free in giving
That he must seem a dull and prosy fool?
   Some claim that when a life like this is done
   It's like the setting of a noble sun.

91

For morals are the measure of a man,
Not what he says, not what the preacher cries.
When he's alone, doing the best he can,
Striving forever for the major prize,
What does he do? How does he really act
When things are going wrong and he is losing?
How does he show himself when facing fact
And every move he makes is of his choosing?
How does he treat his children and his wife,
Has he paid taxes without sly evasion,
And how has he performed in business life?
Is he a foe of snide discrimination?
   The morals of a man should bear inspection
   It's honesty we seek and not perfection.

-92-

The morals of a man are tested weekly,
Temptation comes at him from every road,
And if he handles them supine or meekly
His basic character will soon erode.
Saint James has said it well: 'Not how he prays
'And beats his breast in public, but the way
'He aids the widow and her child, the ways
'He serves the public in his working day.'
What has he done to make his nation better?
Does he trade goods at fair evaluation
And has he shown compassion to a debtor
Or helped a young man find an occupation?
  Pompous or vain your system should not be
  But simple truths that reign eternally.

-93-

Across six decades tense I served my nation
In varied kinds of work and found it thrilling
To be in Washington at duty station
At tasks I liked, so I was more than willing.
Most of the time I was engaged in battle
With communism and its dire effects,
We strove to expedite its sure death rattle
By application of our intellects.
But always as the noose began to tighten
And I could see its imminent demise
My vision of the future seemed to brighten,
Until the Fates bestowed a grand surprise:
    The enmity is gone, now we are brothers,
    A team in league to stabilize the others!

-94-

Why have I fought for civil rights for others?
Because for such great goals we must unite,
Jews, Cath'lics, Baptists, infidels are brothers
All bound together in a noble fight.
I watched as gypsy brothers were tormented
No German there to help or lend a hand—
If once the moral structure has been dented
Corruption rages over all the land.
Our system is a tapestry close knitted,
Hard to create but easy to unravel
And then subject to being counterfeited
By demagogues who rouse their noisy rabble.
  What keen delight, what inner satisfaction
  To watch it running right without infraction.

-95-

When I ran they jibed: 'The same old Tax-and-Spend'
And I accepted their snide accusation
But in my heart the words read: 'Tax-and-Mend'
For I could not conceive how any nation
Could last without a constant close attention
Paid to schools and roads, the arts and health
And vital fields like infant care and pensions.
What else is there to do with excess wealth?
I see taxation as a wise solution
That binds us safely in a brotherhood
Where justice brings escape from revolution,
Insurance for the country's common good.
   Nor do I preach with empty piety
   My wealth I've passed back to society.

———————

I believe this more now than ever and have written a long
book to prove it.

Our village had a terrifying jail,
Huge walls of stone, long aisles of murky cells.
Our school, to let us witness the travail
Of prison, let us visit but the smell
Made me quite sick and drove me to decision:
'I'll ne'er participate in any crime
'That runs the risk of landing me in prison.'
I still retain my fear of serving time.
Years later, after I had kept my vow,
They made a move to knock the old stones down
But sager heads prevailed. They stopped and now
An art museum decorates our town.
   The walls that once performed a penal duty
   Are dedicated now to serving beauty.

-97-

I am opposed to sentences of death,
They are so final, so without recall.
No force should stop another human breath.
Where came this thought? Once in a lecture hall
I heard discussion by a deputy
Who knew the law, and he proved loud and clear
That only poor men hang, the rich go free,
The blacks are lynched as white men domineer.
Were I the legal power of a state
I'd pardon or commute each penalty,
I'd force my government to abdicate
As executioner for villainy.
   Death would be limited to one dire reason:
   The sin against the state, the sin of treason.

Written in Scotland after a study of the inequities of the death penalty there. Confirmed year after year in America.

I've said as governor I'd sign no warrant
Permitting legal forms of execution
Because I deem such punishment abhorrent.
But there *are* crimes beyond my absolution:
The rape of children trustingly enmeshed
In horrors vile. Such sadists should be shot.
A monster kills nine boys and gnaws their flesh.
He should be hanged. A king with power ill-got
Slays nineteen girls avoiding all detection.
His throne should be the state's electric chair.
Demonic crime falls outside my protection—
I am humane, but evil I can't bear.
  If this be contradiction I shan't worry,
    There are some fiends the state should promptly bury.

-99-

Some aspects of my native land perplex me:
Why do we tolerate so many guns?
The gunfights in the streets and schools do vex me
For they kill off our daughters and our sons.
How can a man of stable thought and breeding
Innoculate his arms with poisons fatal
And watch, as veins abused and bleeding
Bespill the truth: he's standing at death's portal?
How dare a nation watch each generation
Of children fail in basic learning skills?
We fall behind more caring, prudent nations,
Inviting devastating social ills.
   How can we be so arrogant, so blind
   To waste our major gift: our country's mind?

———

Pusan, Korea
October 13, 1993

-100-

My passport bears no page denoting Fear!
No map that reads 'Beyond this point be dragons!'
Nor warnings dire that hazards might appear:
'From here prepare to circle all the wagons!'
No 'Care! These lands are swept by insurrection!'
Or 'In this jungle maddened tigers roam!'
But foreign crimes are less than the infection
That we've released right in our cherished home.
A girl of seven on her way to school
Is killed by gunfire from a passing pick-up,
All little boys had better learn life's rule:
'Give muggers all they ask for in a stick-up.'
   No dragons, but one great absurdity:
   'Control of guns means loss of liberty.'

————

Vladivostok
October 11, 1993

-101-

How bold he is! That coat of flaming red,
His golden beak, his all-commanding crest,
The way he preens, the way he holds his head
As if to challenge: 'Am I not the best?'
How proud you must be of your handsome mate!
The way he struts and postures in the sun,
Bright feathers radiant, and each plume ornate
Pronouncing loudly: 'A phenomenon!'
But you, the somber keeper of the nest,
Wear plumage subtler than your Romeo,
Burnt orange, ochre, olive, and the rest
A soft-hued pastel blending all aglow.
   My eyes pass o'er the bold. They feast on you,
   The overwhelming beauty of the two.

Completed at 3:45 in the morning.

-102-

I would not care to be a male today
In age group seventeen to thirty-five,
Confusion in the rules of Yea-and-Nay
Make it too complicated to survive.
The laws of courtship have been changed so rashly
That classic gestures seem a bit absurd.
They cry harassment if a man moves brashly
But if he's reticent he is a nerd.
Young men are trapped in this bizarre confusion
And they opt out, withdrawing from the race.
They seek a refuge in some safe seclusion,
Confused about new rules in nuptial's chase.
   There is a consequence that I am dreading:
   Fine girls will find no partners for their weddings.

The last two lines are trebly relevant since I have in my
home three gorgeous girls who seem to have no chance
of finding husbands.

-103-

Early and late I've been a strong defender
Of *Women's Lib* because I'd seen how brutal
The rules were in the bitter wars of gender
Where women must surmount laws that are feudal.
Her disadvantages in law were massive,
At times she seemed to have no rights whatever.
She was supposed to be demure and passive
(But she could shield herself if she were clever.)
Religions often dealt with her as chattel
And heaped restrictions on each move she made.
Combatting bias is an endless battle—
All equalizing laws must be obeyed.
    What should be rectified the first of all:
    Those stultifying dictates of Saint Paul.

-104-

When I began to write a friend reported:
'Females will give you constant consternation,
'Our language has been savagely distorted
'And thought police wreak added desolation:
'Word *girl* may not be used past sweet sixteen,
'*The fairer sex* is scorned by all the knowing
'And *perfect lady* is downright obscene,
'Banned *weaker sex* shows how the wind is blowing.
'These can't be used. The only phrase allowed,
'*Young woman*, has no useful beat or rhyme
'And still we write it for we have been cowed.
 It grows quite stale but now's used all the time.'
　　Poor women! Writers find it quite a shame—
　　The only sex without a singing name.

―――――――

New York editors can be severe in eliminating words that
seem pejorative to women. They do not unilaterally cut,
but they do counsel strongly against unwise usage.

105

Divorce is like the bursting of a dam
Which spews its muddy waters far and wide
Disclosing that this marriage was a sham,
That promises *to love till death* have died.
The hemorrhage of once related lives,
That looked as if in time they could be blended
Like other bonded husbands and their wives,
Is testament to love that's crudely ended.
Deep scars remain that no one can erase
From wounds so deep they cannot be absolved.
Two fine lives humbled in a cruel disgrace
And injury to everyone involved.
    Divorce is curst, a monumental vice
    To be condemned, and I've been guilty twice.

106

I rarely dream but on the nights they come
I undergo cruel self-evaluations
Until my brain is paralyzed and numb
Reviewing my defeats, humiliations.
I face tough tasks for which I'm not prepared,
Exams for which I have not read the books,
All my deficiencies are known and bared
I cringe at the interrogators' looks.
Far worse my crimes so foul I'm loath to mention,
Deserving universal condemnation,
Then, fleeing to escape my retribution,
I wake with screams and dripping perspiration.
  When I awake I'm glad to be alive
  Not to prevail but merely to survive.

-107-

The devil dreams are not the total story.
With medals, accolades and over-praising
I am allowed my modicum of glory
To a degree that sometimes is amazing.
Each mail brings heady piles of commendations
And testaments to what my books bestow
And scores of tantalizing invitations,
Exciting meetings everywhere I go.
Night is a safeguard against vanity,
Brings caution that such fame is frail and fleeting.
If pampered, fame's a threat to sanity,
A vain indulgence sure to be defeating.
  A subtle team: the day allows elation
    Till night creeps in with counterpoised deflation.

-108-

My doctors cared for me in brilliant fashion
And I gave them a lot of things to do:
A major heart attack, but I'd a passion
To keep on working so they pulled me through.
I asked them for a new hip, they complied
And then a five-part bypass was required,
New teeth, a cure for gout, eyes rectified
Plus half a dozen 'fixes' I desired.
One thing they could not cure, my leg unsteady,
For thirty years I worked in constant pain
But when each morning came I was quite ready
To hurry to my desk and type again.
   Since I was born to work I struggle through it,
   Hold to the plan, ignore the pain, and do it.

―――――――

The fierce pain in my leg began in 1965. The other
medical problems continued for the balance of my life.
Most of these sonnets were written in severe pain.

-109-

I asked both men: 'What is your best prediction
'For this old flesh?' The younger man replied:
'One year.' The older smiled: 'In your affliction
'With proper care two years are on your side.'
 A time too brief, but then a voice commanded:
'Whatever time is left, get back to work
'For Life and Death are always even handed
'In their respect for men who do not shirk.'
 Pile up the tasks, the manuscripts unfinished,
 So much to do, so little time to do it,
 But if one strives with visions undiminished
 He girds his loins and simply battles through it.
    Life's end can be as grand as the beginning
    If one sustains the dream of final winning.

Whence the drive.

To be alive this day is boon sufficient
To marvel at a new sun in the sky
To know that at one's task one is efficient
To hear the lone bird's solitary cry.
I watch the doughty squirrel defend his cache
Against the long-billed birds that try to take it
And cheer when he attacks them with a dash
To drive them back their feathers all atwit.
Beyond our fence there is an infant day school
And all day long I hear the shouts of joy,
It seems a park where youthful chaos rules,
The impish girls, one loud obnoxious boy.
   To watch this flow of life has been most thrilling
   And to participate I'm still quite willing.

-111-

I spend spare change to buy sunflower seed
And toss it on the lawn outside my study
So I can watch the hungry come and feed:
Red robins, rascal squirrels, and the ruddy
Grosbeak's luminescent beak and wing,
The flashing cardinals, a dazzling couple,
Bright glimpse of sky that only bluebirds bring.
Then comes the sly raccoon with long tail supple
The shy opossum with his lumbering gait
Wise owl observing all with somber mood.
This troupe of entertainers for me wait
Because I share with them a little food.
   And as I watch their antics round my tree
   My heart is gladdened and my soul set free.

Always I come back to nature.

- *112* -

L'Envoi

My ship is set to sail to seas unknown
The bo's'n calls my name and I must go.
The bird to guide us on our way has flown
Enticing me to ports I do not know.
Myself when young did eagerly explore
And never stopped till I had reached the moon
Trod Gobi's sands and heard Zambezi's roar,
Spied Bora Bora in her snug lagoon.
I dream of all the glories I have seen
Karnak and Thebes and Angkor, treasures three.
Great Himalayas with their peaks serene
And blood-red Petra steeped in mystery.
    The gods who shared such wonders in the past
    Have surely saved the very best till last.

————

The fifth line is my homage to the sardonic quatrain of
Omar Khayyam:

    Myself when young did eagerly frequent
    Doctor and Saint, and heard great argument
      About it and about: but evermore
    Came out by the same door as in I went.

Appendix

Working on the Sonnets

Working on the Sonnets

Sonnet

To A

Weathered Wanderer

1   The day came when he roamed our roads no more,
2   His heart was willing but his strength declined.
3   His walking stick stood dusty by the door,
4   And neighbors wondered: 'Could it be his mind?'

5   They sent me to inquire and he explained:
6   'To travel far I was ordained at birth.
7   'So do not grieve that now I am enchained,
8   'The soul that soars cannot be bound to earth.

9   'Proust though in bed roamed Paris day and night,
10 'While in his garret Chatterton hatched schemes.
11 'Blind Milton still saw vistas of delight,
12 'And Emily fled Amherst in her dreams.

13   'A mind can tour the world at little cost,
14   'And visions once perceived are never lost.'

I have worked so ardently on these sonnets and over such a long time that I thought it might be interesting for the reader to witness the decisions that arise when one is trying to polish a sonnet grammatically, intellectually and musically. This is game-playing with words.

1. When I finally hit upon '**he roamed our roads**' as a substitute for 'walked our streets' or 'trod our paths' the improvement was instantly obvious.

2. This line was changed repeatedly because it was not effective in its earlier forms.

3. This is one of the two lines which had the least corrupting and the fewest corrections, the only change being 'idle by the door' to 'dusty by the door,' a change of considerable importance. The fortunate repetition of the letter 'd' in **'dusty'** and **'door'** is a real improvement.

4. This underwent frequent change because it represented a dangerous innovation in that it introduced into the body of the sonnet a new group of actors — the neighbors — and this was not an easy adjustment.

5. The same insecurity operated here in that the **'I'** was introduced. But it seemed to me that both of these modifications were justified and I was finally satisfied with the unity of the first five lines.

6. I worked hard to find the proper transition between the first five lines and the body of the sonnet. It was solved by the use of the infinitive **'to travel far'** because that gave me a poetic structure and some words with a poetic resonance.

7. The use here of the word **'enchained'** not only gave me an attractive rhyme for **'explained'** but also an inner rhyme with **'ordained,'** which I think strengthens the sonnet, as if it had three legs upon which to stand and gain strength.

8. This originally read 'the mind that soars,' but that had to be eliminated because of its similarity to line 13. In each case the changed word 'mind' to **'soul'** in 8; and 'soul' to **'mind'** in 13 is stronger. Besides, the repetition of the 's' sound in 8 adds much to the poetic quality of the sonnet.

9. I was from the start enchanted by the felicity of the four lines 9-12. It seemed to me that they came out just right and nailed down the purpose of the sonnet. The citation of the four splendid artists whose lives sent powerful reverberations through the structure of the sonnet added a literary touch which was needed and which added considerably to the artistic merit of the poem. But observe the purely verbal difficulties that these lovely lines encountered. Originally, 9 and 11 read: **'Proust, though in bed,'** and **'Milton, though blind,'** and this wouldn't do. One fine critic objected to the phrase **'While in his garret',** since it implied that Proust and Chatterton were working in roughly the same years, which was not the case.

11. It was easy to get rid of **'Milton, though blind,'** but that induced the repetition of 'saw visions of delight,' which duplicated the word **'visions'** in line 14. **'Vistas'** was a lovely, poetic substitution.

12. This is the only line which remained unchanged during all the years of editing. It is the perfect line in the finished sonnet and the epitome of what the sonnet sought to say. I have spoken of the quiet perfection of line 11, which seems to grow more felicitous with every month that passes.

13-14. The final couplet is appropriate for this sonnet if the phrase '**A mind can tour**' and '**visions**' can be protected from repetition.